Beatrix Potter's
DERWENTWATER

Beatrix Potter's
DERWENTWATER

Wynne Bartlett and Joyce Irene Whalley

With original illustrations by
BEATRIX POTTER

FREDERICK WARNE

914.2787
B24, b

FREDERICK WARNE

Published by the Penguin Group
27 Wrights Lane, London W8 5TZ, England
Viking Penguin Inc., 40 West 23rd Street, New York, New York 10010, U.S.A.
Penguin Books Australia Ltd, Ringwood, Victoria, Australia
Penguin Books Canada Ltd, 2801 John Street, Markham, Ontario, Canada L3R 1B4
Penguin Books (N.Z.) Ltd, 182–190 Wairau Road, Auckland 10, New Zealand

Penguin Books Ltd, Registered Offices: Harmondsworth, Middlesex, England

First published 1988

Text copyright © Joyce Irene Whalley and Wynne Bartlett, 1988
Beatrix Potter's original illustrations copyright © Frederick Warne & Co.

British Cataloguing in Publication Data
Bartlett, Wynne
    Beatrix Potter's Derwentwater.
    1. Potter, Beatrix—Homes and haunts—England—Derwentwater Region
    2. Derwentwater Region (England)—Description and travel—Guide-books
    I. Title   II. Whalley, Joyce Irene
    914.27'87   PR6031.072Z/

    ISBN 0–7232–3312–8

Designed by Yvonne Dedman

Set in Linotron Trump Mediaeval by
Rowland Phototypesetting Ltd, Bury St Edmunds, Suffolk
Printed and bound in Great Britain by
William Clowes Limited, Beccles and London

Frontispiece: Beatrix Potter with Kep in 1913
Title page: A sketch by Beatrix of the view across
Derwentwater to St. Herbert's Island, 1903

*Dedicated to all who love
the Derwentwater area*

Contents

A map showing the three walks is on page 48

Acknowledgements

The authors would like to express their appreciation of the help given by Mrs. Enid Wilson of Keswick, whose wide-ranging knowledge of the area and its people was so freely given and so gratefully received. We are also greatly indebted to Mrs. Miranda Pemberton-Pigott of Fawe Park, and Lord Rochdale of Lingholm, for so kindly allowing us access to Beatrix Potter's holiday houses and gardens. We should also like to thank Miss Marjorie Dymock and Mr. and Mrs. Dunn for their helpfulness during our visits to Lingholm and Fawe Park, and Mrs. Willow Taylor and her colleagues at Hill Top for their kind co-operation.

Thanks are also due to the National Trust, who are the owners of the Derwentwater sketchbook.

Introduction

IT is a constant surprise and delight to Lake District visitors to discover that Beatrix Potter anchored her characters firmly in real Lakeland countryside. Using the clues left by Beatrix Potter in her books, it is possible to start on a fascinating detective quest through Derwentwater, following the trail of little Lucie to Mrs. Tiggy-winkle, visiting 'Owl Island', where Squirrel Nutkin lost his tail, walking close to the old stone wall where Mr. Benjamin Bunny smoked his pipe.

For ten years between 1885 and 1907, the Potter family spent their long summer holidays on the shores of Derwentwater. Beatrix's holiday sketchbook for the summer of 1903 (referred to in this book as 'the Derwentwater sketchbook') survives, full of detailed preparatory drawings and watercolour sketches. Many of these sketches formed the backgrounds to the finished illustrations in three of her best-loved books: *The Tale of Squirrel Nutkin, The Tale of Benjamin Bunny,* and *The Tale of Mrs. Tiggy-Winkle.*

Material from the Derwentwater sketchbook has been available previously in a limited facsimile edition only – this is the first time that visitors to the Lake District have been able to see the original sketches on which Beatrix Potter based her most famous books and to use the sketches as clues in piecing together the real world that her characters inhabited.

Beatrix was not the only Potter with artistic talent: her brother Bertram was a competent painter, and her father Rupert was a very fine photographer. This book includes not only Beatrix's drawings and finished illustrations but also the work of other members of her family, forming a unique and fascinating record of Derwentwater at the turn of the century. With this book as a guide, the visitor can enter the real world of Squirrel Nutkin, Mrs. Tiggy-winkle and Benjamin Bunny, a world very little changed since Beatrix Potter, on the brink of a famous career, sat sketching in the summer of 1903.

Beatrix Potter

(1866–1943)

Beatrix Potter, aged eight, and her parents

B EATRIX POTTER was born on 28 July 1866, the only daughter and elder child of well-to-do parents. Her father, Rupert Potter (1832–1914), although trained as a barrister, led the life of a gentleman of leisure, and her mother, Helen Potter (1839–1932), followed the usual round of the leisured ladies of her class and time.

For almost the first six years of her life Beatrix was an only child, and even after the birth of her brother Bertram in 1872 she led an isolated life. The children's nursery was cut off at the top of the house in Bolton Gardens, London; other children were not encouraged to visit, and they appear to have had few or no friends.

Comparatively little is known about Beatrix Potter's early family life. There exist a few letters to and from her father, which indicate a pleasant and loving relationship, but nothing survives of her dealings with her mother, and one is forced to conclude that her children were of little interest to Mrs. Potter. In the *Journal*, started when Beatrix was thirteen and written in code, we catch a glimpse of her charming friendship with the elderly Mr. Gaskell, widower of the writer Mrs. Elizabeth Gaskell, and of her great love for her grandmother. But we hear of her mother only when Beatrix felt she was being difficult.

Although they had both wealth and leisure, the Potters did not form part of the old aristocracy, since their wealth came originally from trade. This and their North Country origins set them apart from certain sections of London society. They were further separated from the life around them by the fact that the family were Unitarians and so did not participate in the various yearly festivals and events such as Christmas. However, Rupert Potter was fond of outdoor pursuits, especially shooting and fishing, so that although part of the year was spent in London, he followed the English practice of removing his family to the country during the summer months. As he was not a member of

The view from the back garden of the Potters' home in Bolton
Gardens in Kensington, London

the landed gentry, Rupert Potter had to rent his summer resi-
dences from year to year, frequently selecting houses in Scotland or the Lake District. For the Potter children the contrast
between the restricted life that was theirs for most of the year
and the freedom of the unspoilt countryside around their holiday homes must have been forceful indeed. On Beatrix the
result was profound. Painting and sketching appear to have been
the earliest occupations of the young Beatrix, to judge from her
childhood sketchbooks which have survived.

She might have expressed her imaginative feelings by writing
– as did the Brontës. Instead she painted and drew, and since her
London life offered only restricted subject matter, she was
drawn instinctively to the natural world for interest and inspiration. If human friends were unwelcome in the Potter nursery,
rabbits, mice and similar creatures were not – perhaps the Potter

Above: Pages from nine-year-old Beatrix's sketchbook
Below: Beatrix's pet rabbit, painted when she was about thirteen

Beatrix and her brother Bertram, photographed by their father in 1878

The Potter family at Wray Castle, near Windermere

parents felt these were less disturbing to the quiet tenor of the household. So Beatrix and her brother studied and drew their pets, and when the family migrated for the summer months to Scotland or the Lake District their interests were further stimulated by the countryside around them.

Always shy and reserved, Beatrix Potter found in natural history an absorbing interest. It was one that could be followed up in solitude, when she could make her own independent observations and she could draw what she saw. But Beatrix's interest in art and in nature, and her artistic ability, were not without their foundations in her own family.

Above: A pencil sketch by Rupert Potter of a group of dogs
Opposite: Two pages from Rupert Potter's sketchbook, dated 1853

Her father, Rupert Potter, may have had a greater influence on his daughter than has generally been accepted. His surviving early sketchbook (now part of the Linder Bequest in the Victoria and Albert Museum) shows him to have had considerable talent, and he was a regular visitor to the major London art galleries, usually taking the young Beatrix with him. In 1883 they visited the Winter Exhibition at the Royal Academy, and Beatrix was brought face to face for the first time with old masters such as Van Dyck, Gainsborough and Reynolds. 'I never thought there *could* be such pictures,' she enthused to her *Journal.*

From the time of her earliest gallery visits, Beatrix compiled detailed criticisms of what she saw and must have discussed with her father. In her secret writings at least she was not afraid to comment, inspect and consider, and as a result she undoubtedly learnt much from her exhibition visiting, which became a regular part of her London life.

It was her father who must have encouraged her interest in natural history as well as gallery visiting. His early sketchbook in the Victoria and Albert Museum contains a number of sketches of birds and animals, and Beatrix appears to have started off in a style similar to her father's early work, which may have been based, in the case of each artist, on contemporary engravings in books. The early drawings of both Beatrix and her brother suggest that a certain amount of copying was done and that Mr. Potter's library provided the source of these copies. The majority of them were taken from books of natural history, evidence that Rupert Potter was also interested in the topic that was to prove of such importance in his daughter's life.

One important influence in Beatrix Potter's artistic life was her father's close friendship with the successful painter John Everett Millais. As a result of this, she had first-hand and regular experience of a living artist, his work, his life and his public. Even here she was not prepared to accept the world's opinion of Millais' merit but considered each of his paintings for herself, often commenting critically on one or other of his works. Nevertheless, since he knew her work and advised on her artistic studies this family friendship was significant.

There were disadvantages, however, in having a famous artist almost 'in the family'. In 1884 Beatrix wrote of her father, who was critical of some paintings they had gone to view:

> He has not the slightest idea of the difficulty of painting a picture: he can draw very well, but he has hardly attempted watercolour and never oil. A person in this state, with a correct eye and good taste . . . sees all the failures but not the difficulties. He has never stared at a model till he did not know whether it was standing on its feet or its head. Then seeing Mr. Millais paint so often and so easily would make a man hard on other painters. It prevents me showing much of my attempts to him, and I lose much by it.

Apart from the influence of regular visits to galleries and the family involvement with the work of Millais, there was one other important artist whose work both Beatrix Potter and her

One of the many photographs of his friend, the painter John Everett Millais (left), taken by Rupert Potter. By the use of delayed action, he has cleverly included himself in this one

father greatly admired. This was Randolph Caldecott (1846–86). Caldecott was a painter and book illustrator and one, moreover, with a deep love of the countryside and the creatures that inhabit it. Rupert Potter collected Caldecott's work, and two illustrations from one of his children's books still hang at Hill Top (Beatrix Potter's Lake District farm, now owned by the National Trust) and still bear the frame-maker's label to show that they originally came from the old Potter home in London.

The precise amount of influence that the work of Caldecott had on Beatrix Potter's is difficult to assess. Sometimes there is a direct hint, as in *A frog he would a-wooing go* (1883), where in Caldecott's illustrations we can see clearly the shape of the future Mr. Jeremy Fisher. In the many farmyard and country scenes too there are touches that can be recognized later in the younger artist's work – even something of Caldecott's attention to the layout of the text and its relation to the pictorial page can be glimpsed in Beatrix Potter's own books.

Rupert Potter did not paint, but he was a keen photographer, and Beatrix later took up photography with enthusiasm, the two of them going off on expeditions weighed down with the heavy equipment of the period. Rupert Potter frequently photographed models and scenes for Millais, and so Beatrix too learned the method by which she could preserve summer subjects for winter painting. But Rupert also photographed scenes for their own intrinsic beauty and in his choice and composition showed himself to be a photographer of no mean talent. It is probable that, although she was ready to appreciate the use of artistic

Left: From *A Frog He Would a-Wooing Go,* by Randolph Caldecott. Both Beatrix and her father admired the work of this artist and there is no doubt that he was an important influence on Beatrix's later work
Right: A preliminary sketch of Mr. Jeremy Fisher

So off he set with his opera-hat,
Heigho, says ROWLEY!

A photograph of Tenby by Rupert Potter

licence in many of her paintings, Beatrix learnt much of the art of composition through the medium of photography, and its discipline must have affected the way in which she came to look upon the landscapes she chose to paint.

Although it was through her father that Beatrix received the most important influences on her art, both her brother and her mother were able to provide further stimulus. Bertram had always shared Beatrix's interests in natural history and sketching, and later became a full-time artist. Of her mother's work little is known, but one or two paintings survive to show that she was certainly a competent watercolour painter, as were many young ladies of that period, when painting in watercolours was considered an essential accomplishment. But

Mrs. Helen Potter, Beatrix's mother

Below: A watercolour by Mrs. Potter

Mrs. Potter's surviving works date apparently from after her marriage, suggesting that she was sufficiently interested to carry on with her painting, and she too appears to have done the rounds of the art galleries.

Beatrix Potter's background certainly encouraged her to take an interest in art, and painting in particular, and her circumstances led her to study and to persevere with it. She followed a course of drawing lessons, as recommended by Millais, but it was not a success. She realized that technique was something that could be learnt, but that in itself it was not enough. She was always conscious of the desire to express in artistic terms whatever appealed to her, but she appreciated that she often lacked the ability to do so.

> It's all the same, drawing, painting, modelling – the irresistible desire to copy any beautiful object which strikes the eye. Why cannot one be content to look at it? . . . No word about my painting just now, and I don't want any except for more time. I don't want lessons, I want practice.

Beatrix's copy of a lithograph by Sir Edwin Landseer of a dead stag

It might be supposed that a young unmarried girl of prosperous family would not have lacked time for her painting. But there is no doubt that Beatrix Potter's mother was very demanding and expected her somewhat unconventional daughter to behave, in public at least, in the way that other young ladies did. So Beatrix was endlessly absorbed in her mother's round of visits and shopping and servant problems. The regular summer removal was also a great upheaval, in which Beatrix inevitably became involved as she grew older; the *Journal* indicates that Mrs. Potter was extremely difficult to please in the matter of holiday houses.

Although Beatrix may have given the impression in public that she was shy and had little to say in company, her *Journal* belies this reading of her character. It is full of lively accounts of social and political events of the day, indicating not only her uncommon awareness of such things but also that such topics were regularly discussed in the Potter household.

In spite of their predominantly town-oriented life, there is no doubt that both Beatrix and Bertram were naturally attracted to country life. Even in London they managed to keep pets – and not just 'town' pets such as dogs and cats but also rabbits, mice, hedgehogs, even bats, which all found their way to the top floor at Bolton Gardens. In the country this restricted interest could be given wider scope, and the opportunities thus offered to study animals and plants in their natural habitat were taken up eagerly. In Beatrix Potter's *Journal* we read of the variety of wild

From the ages of fifteen to thirty Beatrix Potter kept a journal in her own private code which was not solved until 1958. This extract is the start of Psalm 90

Beatrix and Bertram with their pet dog

and semi-wild creatures that they studied and drew and that replaced, for these rather isolated children, the more normal companionship of young friends.

For Bertram there was some escape; he went off to school, and as he grew older, Beatrix enjoyed his companionship only during the school holidays. She herself studied under various governesses, as was usual for girls of her class at that date, and there were no friends with whom she could share lessons. She became to some extent an only child again, as she had been in the years before Bertram's birth.

Bertram Potter with one of his own paintings. The photograph was probably taken by his father at Lingholm

Bertram's years away at school gave him one great advantage over his sister – he was able to begin that break with parental control over his movements which it took Beatrix more than thirty years to achieve. Bertram decided to be an artist, and an artist he became. Leaving the family, he settled in Scotland to practise his art, maintaining only tenuous links with his parents and sister. He later married secretly and spent the rest of his life farming in the Scottish Borders.

Beatrix's solitariness obviously stimulated her interest in things she could do on her own, and chief among these was drawing and painting. Her long summer holidays amid beautiful scenery provided her with endless subjects, although she was also able to find topics among the everyday things around her, from antique chairs to flower-pots. Equally important for the future development of her art were the many studies she made of the small animals she adopted as pets, showing them in every mood and from all angles until she was fully satisfied that she had captured the true essence of each creature.

It is probable that at first Beatrix did not consciously set out to become an artist. Her main interest was in *recording* what she saw, and it was her desire for skill in accurate delineation that

Studies of chairs, drawn
by Beatrix Potter when the
family were on holiday at
Fawe Park in 1903

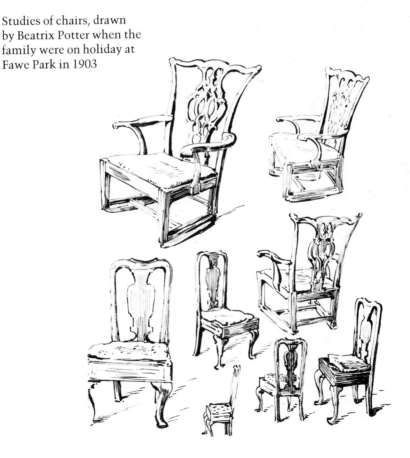

Above: A group of brown mushrooms (*Amanita aspera*)
Opposite above: Lithographs of a privet hawk moth and caterpillar by
Beatrix Potter, showing magnified sections of wing scales
Opposite below: A sketch by Beatrix of a magnified water flea, 1887

encouraged her to take her only drawing lessons. Her scientific
accuracy is nowhere better seen than in her paintings of fungi,
which have been used to illustrate a standard book on the
subject. Yet these highly skilled renderings are also works of
great beauty. Her microscopic work is artistically attractive as
well as being technically correct. It is obvious that, for her,
drawing and painting were almost as essential as eating and
sleeping. Even when she had long given up producing children's
books, she would still paint or sketch for her own pleasure, just
as, long before she had ever thought of publication, she had filled
numerous sketchbooks with all that caught her eye as she went
about with her parents.

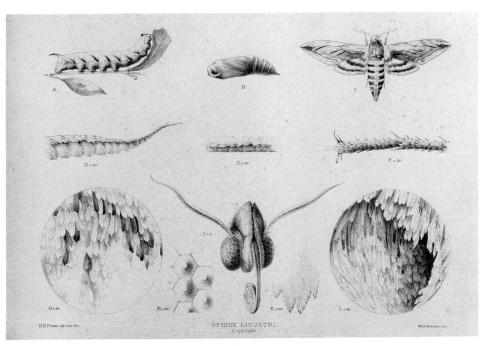

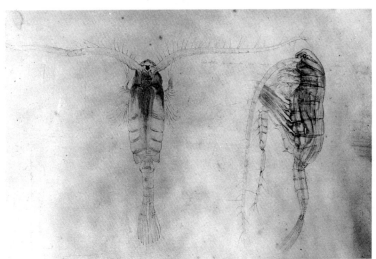

A happy New Year to you.

Hildesheimer & Faulkner. Copyright   Designed in England. Printed in Germany

One of Beatrix's greeting cards, published by Hildesheimer and
Faulkner in 1890

'A game of cards' – one of Beatrix's miniature-style paintings

Like most artists, Beatrix Potter's style changed considerably over the years as her own art matured and as fashions changed. Her very earliest work was based on the style of book illustration most familiar to her in her youth. The pictures would have been engraved in black and white on wood, copper or steel for the most part, though her father's library probably also contained natural history books with coloured plates. Her first published works were very much in the style of contemporary chromolitho illustrations popular for children's books and greetings cards. In these her colouring was muted; the soft greys and fawns, and even the reds and greens, appeared subdued. Indeed, her original artwork looks just like the finished product of many of the cheaper publishers of the period – but with a significant difference: the work surviving from this date indicates an extremely accomplished artist, producing exquisite miniature-style paintings and using a very dry and delicate brush technique – to which most of the reproductions sadly failed to do justice.

Towards the end of the century, no doubt as a result of her increasing interest in landscape, we find a much more fluent style of painting evolving. Beatrix was still using watercolour but in a much thinner form and with brighter colours. She frequently also used sepia ink in conjunction with her painting at this period, giving the subjects a firm but somewhat broken outline, as if she saw the two media, ink and watercolour, as equally essential. Her surviving work also indicates just how much practice went into the final depiction of any one of the creatures that appeared in her books. Many sheets of paper survive, covered with pencil sketches of cats, rabbits or mice in every possible pose, and the same is true of dozens of other birds or animals that she chose to represent. And the sketches show not only complete subjects but also limbs or heads or tails, drawn again and again, until she was sure that she had the movement right and was ready to transfer her studies to the final watercolour.

It was not until she was about twenty-four that she began to think of using her art commercially. By then she was very conscious of her dependence on her parents and of their determination that she should remain dependent. Money offered at least some kind of freedom, and that might be obtained by the one thing she had to sell – her skill as an artist. So Beatrix set about submitting her drawings to London publishers. It was not easy for her, and her earliest works did not find ready acceptance, but eventually some of her Christmas card designs were bought and published by the firm of Hildesheimer and Faulkner in 1890.

Now things began to fall into place for Beatrix. She had long been fond of her old governess's children and visited them in Wandsworth whenever she could. In 1893 she wrote a picture-letter to Noel, the youngest, who was ill, embellishing it with little sketches, to his great delight. Other similar letters to children followed, and, no doubt to her own surprise, Beatrix discovered in herself a gift for imaginative story-telling to match her artistic talent.

Her big chance came with the first of the *Peter Rabbit* books. In 1901 she decided to make a book out of the picture-letter that she had sent some years before to Noel Moore. As this first attempt was rejected by all the publishers to whom it was sent,

Opposite: Pen and ink sketches of sheep and cows

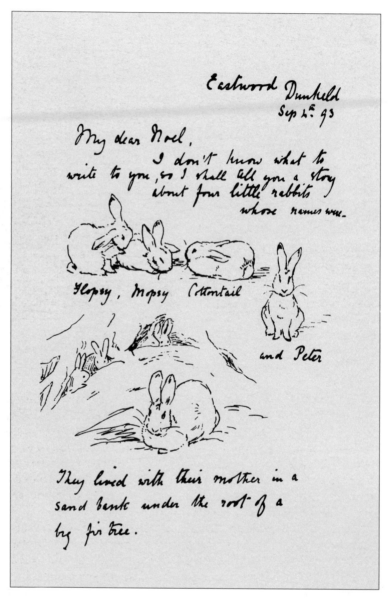

Beatrix's 'Peter Rabbit' picture letter to Noel Moore

Left: The first edition of *The Tale of Peter Rabbit*, published by
Frederick Warne in 1902
Right: Norman Warne, Beatrix's main contact at Frederick Warne

she decided to publish it herself, but while this private edition
was in production one of the publishers offered to reconsider
his decision. The original black-and-white illustrations were
coloured, a number of changes were made in the text, and in
1902 Frederick Warne published *The Tale of Peter Rabbit* in the
form in which it was to conquer the world – and thus initiated a
long and fruitful partnership between the publisher and the
artist, as one little book succeeded another.

Her increasing fame and financial independence at first made
little impact on Beatrix Potter's life. She remained tied to her
parents' apron-strings, going wherever they wished and when,
regardless of her own desires. Moreover, as she grew older
Beatrix found to her dismay that she was in demand over
household matters too because her mother expected more and

more assistance from her unmarried grown-up daughter. Her father was undoubtedly proud of her achievements and had copies of her works especially bound for his own library, but as his health failed he too became almost as unmanageable and demanding as her mother. The gleam of hope that was vouchsafed to Beatrix was all too quickly extinguished. In 1905, against her parents' wishes, she had accepted a proposal of marriage from Norman Warne, a member of the publishing family with whom she had developed pleasantly informal as well as business relations. Sadly, he died suddenly of leukaemia within weeks of the engagement, and Beatrix was if anything worse off than before. The little books which had proved so popular continued to be published by Warne, although Beatrix found visiting her publisher's office was an acutely painful reminder of happier occasions when Norman was alive.

She immersed herself in her writing and drawing as a welcome relief. The sketch books clearly show the mastery she had obtained over her art by this time, for it must be remembered that the sketchbook paintings were done on the spot, and watercolour, unlike oils, does not allow for retouching. In view of this fact, the finished quality of many of her sketches is remarkable. It was small wonder, therefore, that when she set herself to paint the final pictures for her books, she produced work of a very high quality indeed. She was able to combine her love for the detailed delineation of birds and animals with the great sweep of landscape or the more homely intimacy of gardens. Much of the detail in her finished book work can be traced to earlier sketches – a gate, a fence, a pot of flowers, a forest glade – sometimes painted merely for the pleasure she took in the object or the view, sometimes collected consciously for use in a book then in preparation. As a result, in much of her work, however fantastic the story and the protagonists, the background is firmly anchored in reality, and often a recognizable reality at that.

As she grew older, Beatrix Potter's style became much more impressionistic, especially when painting purely for her own pleasure. She made less use of outline, except for a faint pencil touch now and then to guide her brush. In one of her books,

A study of carnations painted by Beatrix Potter in the summer of 1903 at Fawe Park

One of the rough pen-and-ink sketches for *The Tale of Mr. Tod*,
published in 1912

however, published as late as 1912, she showed a very different,
and rather uncharacteristic, style. This was *The Tale of Mr. Tod*,
in which black-and-white illustration is far more prominent
than watercolour. The rather heavy pen-and-ink drawings were
sometimes enclosed within a frame, giving the impression of
woodcuts. The whole appearance of this book was quite unlike
anything she had produced before – or was to repeat in later
books. Nevertheless the result was not so far removed from
certain aspects of contemporary style, since it carried overtones
of the type of work done by certain artists for the private presses
of the period, and in particular Lucien Pissarro's Eragny Press. It
seems that Beatrix Potter continued to be aware of the artistic
trends of the day and to be influenced, at least to a modified
degree, by these trends.

Beatrix had begun to invest her money in property in her
beloved Lake District – something her father approved of as long
as she had nothing to do with the property herself. But as
gradually more and more land was acquired, her presence on
the spot became necessary. A way towards independence was
opening up for her, and in 1913, at the age of forty-seven, Beatrix
Potter married William Heelis, the solicitor who had handled

Beatrix Potter and William Heelis on their wedding day

her business affairs in the Lake District. From then on she began a new and absorbing life as Mrs. Heelis, Lake District farmer and sheep breeder, turning her back on her old life and all it had meant for so long. Her father died in 1914 but her mother lived until 1932, and for many years she too was provided with a house in the Lake District – but not too near Mrs. Heelis!

Little literary or artistic work came out of Beatrix Potter's later years, though she still continued to paint and draw for her own pleasure in spite of failing eyesight. But there were no more Peter Rabbit books. Beatrix Heelis died during the dark and difficult days of the Second World War, in 1943, better known among her neighbours as a breeder of Herdwick sheep and a somewhat irascible old lady than as the creator of the enchanted and enchanting world of Peter Rabbit and his friends.

Opposite: Beatrix Potter discussing sheep at the Woolpack Show, Eskdale
Right: A line illustration from the privately printed *The Tale of Peter Rabbit,* published in 1901

Walks around Derwentwater

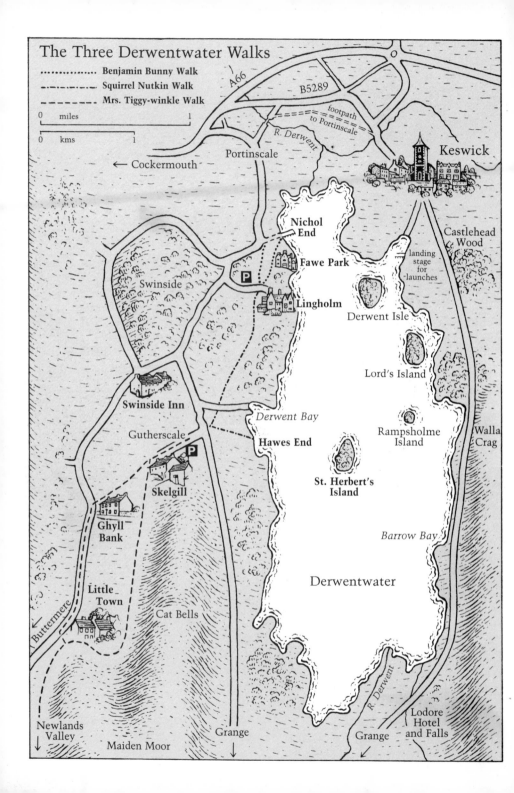

The Three Derwentwater Walks

.... Benjamin Bunny Walk
—··—··— Squirrel Nutkin Walk
— — — — Mrs. Tiggy-winkle Walk

0   miles   1

0   kms   1

A66

B5289

footpath to Portinscale

R. Derwent

Portinscale

Keswick

← Cockermouth

Castlehead Wood

Nichol End

Fawe Park

landing stage for launches

P

Swinside

Lingholm

Derwent Isle

Lord's Island

Swinside Inn

Derwent Bay

Rampsholme Island

Walla Crag

Gutherscale

Hawes End

P

Skelgill

St. Herbert's Island

Ghyll Bank

Barrow Bay

Little Town

Derwentwater

Cat Bells

Buttermere

R. Derwent

Newlands Valley ↓

Grange ↓

Grange ↓

Lodore Hotel and Falls

Maiden Moor

1 An aerial view of Derwentwater

Benjamin Bunny and Fawe Park

2 *above left:* The first page of the Derwentwater sketchbook, showing the retaining wall of the upper orchard with its buttresses. Peter and Benjamin climb down this wall with the help of the pear tree in *The Tale of Benjamin Bunny*
3 *above right:* Another sketch of the buttressed wall, showing the stone slabs which form the top of the wall. The sketch shows a bee-hive standing in the angle of the wall
4 *left:* The wall and pear tree today

5 A close-up sketch of the pear tree, together with the corresponding picture from *The Tale of Benjamin Bunny*

6 A background study of the top of the wall, for the book illustration showing old Mr. Benjamin Bunny 'prancing along the top of the wall of the upper terrace . . . smoking a pipe of rabbit tobacco'

7 *opposite above:* Derwentwater from Fawe Park, dated 'Sept. 3 '03'
8 *opposite below:* This page from the Derwentwater sketchbook shows the view from the top of the wall towards Derwentwater and the fells on the east side of the lake. The tree-covered island is Derwent Island, with the slopes of Walla Crag behind it

9 *right:* Peter Rabbit and Benjamin Bunny standing on top of the wall looking down into the vegetable garden
10 *below:* Derwentwater from Fawe Park today

11 *opposite:* Sketches of the vegetable garden at Fawe Park, showing the planks along which Peter and Benjamin walked carrying their stolen onions

12 *above:* The vegetable garden below the wall, where Mr. McGregor had his scarecrow and the corresponding book picture from *The Tale of Benjamin Bunny*

Squirrel Nutkin and Lingholm

13 A page from the Derwentwater sketchbook, showing Derwentwater and St. Herbert's Island from Derwent Bay

14 Background painting for *The Tale of Squirrel Nutkin* from Beatrix Potter's 1901 sketchbook, and the finished book illustration, in which the squirrels sail over to 'Owl Island' to gather nuts

15 A page from the 1901 sketchbook, inscribed by Beatrix Potter 'Derwent Bay – between Lingholm and Cat Bells, where Nutkin set sail!' The finished book illustration shows the squirrels making their rafts

16 An oak tree from the 1901 sketchbook, which Beatrix Potter used as the home of Old Brown, the owl

17 A background sketch, again dated 1901, showing a tree on the shore of Derwent Bay, with St. Herbert's Island in the distance, and the finished illustration showing the squirrels filling their sacks with nuts

18 *opposite above:* This painting from the Derwentwater sketchbook shows St. Herbert's Island against the background of Walla Crag, with Falcon Crag on the right. Cat Ghyll runs between them
19 *opposite below:* The same scene, unchanged today

20 *above:* A painting by Beatrix Potter of the main staircase inside the house at Lingholm
21 *right:* These squirrels sitting on a log were painted from the two squirrels bought by Beatrix as models for *The Tale of Squirrel Nutkin*

Mrs. Tiggy-winkle and the Newlands Valley

22 The Newlands Valley path today

23 *left:* The Newlands Valley from the Derwentwater sketchbook. In the book, Lucie is shown running along a steep path with this view in front of her and Little-town below. Beatrix Potter exercised some artistic licence in placing Little Town so far up the Newlands Valley, but the head of the valley is easily recognizable

24 The Derwentwater sketchbook view of the path from Little Town to Manse Gate. In the illustration from *The Tale of Mrs. Tiggy-Winkle*, Lucie is seen sitting on a stile of a kind still to be seen in the district, and looking up this same path

25 A waterfall and pool from the Derwentwater sketchbook, which was probably the inspiration for Mrs. Tiggy-winkle's spring, as shown above

26 *above:* A page from the
Derwentwater sketchbook,
showing the path which starts at
Gutherscale and runs above Little
Town, along the lower slopes of
Cat Bells
27 *left:* Lucie and Mrs.
Tiggy-winkle walking along this
path

28 *opposite above left:* Skiddaw
from the slopes of Cat Bells or
from Maiden Moor, as painted in
the Derwentwater sketchbook
29 *opposite above right:* Skiddaw
from Cat Bells
30 *opposite below:* A sketch of the
Newlands Valley by Beatrix Potter

31 *left:* Page 73 of the Derwentwater sketchbook, dated 'Sept. 15', showing the Newlands Valley with Newlands Church in a group of trees, the bridge over Newlands Beck and a farmhouse. The church and the bridge can still be seen from the path near Little Town, although many more trees now surround the bridge and hide it when they are in full leaf. Although Little Town is the nearest group of buildings to the bridge it is not possible to find a viewpoint where the church, bridge and farmhouse can be seen in the relationship shown in the sketch

32 *below:* Newlands Church and the bridge over Newlands Beck today

DERWENTWATER is one of the most northerly of the English Lakes and also one of the widest. At its northern end lies the only town, Keswick. All around the lake the mountains draw close to the water, though less so on the western shores, where lie the two houses, Lingholm and Fawe Park, which the Potter family took for their summer holidays between 1885 and 1907.

Behind the western shores of Derwentwater the scenery is dominated by the great mass of Cat Bells, and this was to be the scene of Lucie's adventures with Mrs. Tiggy-winkle. Further west lies a great valley, Newlands, watched over by steep fells on all sides. Even today it is comparatively remote, and in 1903 it must have been still more so. But it obviously had great attractions for Beatrix Potter, since many of her sketchbook drawings depict scenes at various points between the lake and Newlands valley, which itself forms an important background to the Mrs. Tiggy-winkle drawings. There are still very few houses in the area. In the autumn it is ablaze with colour, the gold and russets of the bracken and the trees set against the stark upper slopes of the fells and the grey stone walls. There are still roads and paths to be followed to the old mine workings. Here Lucie found the door into the hillside – and indeed such holes still exist, though seemingly empty now of miners and hedgehogs alike.

The whole area around Derwentwater offered the artist every possible choice of subject. On wet days (and there are many in the Lake District) Beatrix could sketch the inside of the house and the furniture. As the weather improved, the garden implements and the potting shed provided further variety. And there were expeditions to Keswick.

The Potters seem to have visited the further side of the lake only rarely, being content, for the most part, with their own western shores. On occasion, however, like other tourists then and now, they made excursions. In 1885 Beatrix writes in her *Journal*:

> Went to Buttermere by Grange, Honister and back by Newlands. Extraordinary and striking drive, but one to make one thankful to see a field of corn; an awful road. Never knew what jolting was before, three of the party including self excessively ill following night; recommend said excursion as a cure for colic.

Even today the Honister Pass may hold terrors for the nervous motorist, and we can only imagine what the journey must have been like in a horse-drawn vehicle without pneumatic tyres.

Opposite above: Fawe Park
Opposite below: Lingholm

Left: An old oak cupboard, drawn by Beatrix Potter at Fawe Park in 1903

Above: A sketch of Keswick Market, showing the Moot Hall in
the background, from Beatrix Potter's Derwentwater sketchbook
Opposite above: Keswick Market at the turn of the century
Opposite below: Keswick and the Moot Hall today

Keswick, however, was another matter. It was the nearest
place for shopping, and Beatrix must have visited it often. But
she made very few sketches of it, apart from the scenes in the
Derwentwater sketchbook.

Keswick's Saturday market has been in existence since 1276,
when a charter to hold a market was granted by Edward I. It
continues to be held to the present day – looking much the same
as it did on Saturday, 19 September 1903, when Beatrix Potter

Lavender
bottle

sketched it. We are given the impression that the artist wandered around the bustling market-place unobtrusively, making a quick note of a stall here and a crowd there. It seems likely, from the way the sketches are grouped together, that they were all done on the same day.

Keswick is still quite recognizable from Beatrix Potter's sketches, though the Moot Hall, which dominates the market square and was once the Butter Market, is now the Tourist Office – nor did Beatrix have to contend with cars as well as crowds! The pictures she drew in the market square are especially interesting because of the number of people in them. Her rendering of the human figure was rarely very successful, as she herself was the first to confess. However, in this instance it would appear that as long as she did not try too hard for perfection, she was well able to catch the life and movement of people going about their business and gossiping over their marketing. These rough sketches – especially those of children – have about them a charming spontaneity that compares favourably with the more stilted drawings of Lucie in *The Tale of Mrs. Tiggy-Winkle.*

Sketches of people and stalls at Keswick Market, again from Beatrix Potter's sketch-book of Derwentwater

Above: The Newlands Valley showing Dalehead and Robinson Fells
Opposite above: The Newlands Valley
Opposite below: Looking up the valley to the Honister Pass

Perhaps the reason why Beatrix Potter made so few sketches of Keswick was that she did not like the town. In a letter of 17 February 1929, advising an American friend, Mrs. Marion Perry, about the best places to stay in the Lake District, she wrote: 'Keswick I consider an awfully dull cold town.' The many visitors who throng its streets during the holiday season would hardly agree, and, above all, Keswick is an excellent centre for exploring the north-west area of the Lake District.

When the busy scenes of country-town life palled, there were quiet walks through the woods and down to the lakeside. And when the weather settled fair, as it seems to have done in mid-September 1903, there were longer expeditions into the hills and scrambles up the slopes to find just the right elements of composition – expeditions that have fixed for ever that fine autumn at the turn of the century in a series of watercolour drawings and sketches.

On the last page of the Derwentwater sketchbook Beatrix Potter has lightly pencilled these words:

Mrs. Tiggy Winkle   Newlands
Fawe Park   Benjamin Bunny
Derwentwater   Squirrel Nutkin

She was right to link the books so closely with the scenes depicted in them, for Beatrix Potter was very much an artist of place. In her books the charm of the characters themselves tends to overshadow the fact that every one of them is set firmly in an identifiable landscape. It was the Derwentwater area that inspired some of the finest scenic backgrounds as well as three of the most delightful of all Beatrix Potter's stories.

Unfortunately her *Journal* comes to an end before the majority of the Derwentwater holidays took place, so we have only a few descriptions of her travels in the area. But we do have the 1903 sketchbook to fill in some of the gaps. Today we can still visit the scenes Beatrix Potter sketched that summer and used in her famous books.

The following sections describe three Lakeland expeditions into Beatrix Potter countryside. The walks are easy; the instructions are clear; and each chapter, as well as the colour pages in the centre of the book, is filled with illustrations that will guide you on your trail of detection of Potter landmarks. Perhaps you will see the descendants of Squirrel Nutkin, Mrs. Tiggy-winkle and Benjamin Bunny – they may still be there.

Enjoy yourself.

Opposite above: Stable Hills and the Jaws of Borrowdale from Castlehead Wood
Opposite below: Derwentwater and Cat Bells from Castlehead Wood

General Information

Most of the beautiful Derwentwater countryside in which
Beatrix Potter set the *Tale of Benjamin Bunny, Squirrel
Nutkin,* and *Mrs. Tiggy-Winkle* can be seen and enjoyed from
public footpaths that are within easy reach of Keswick. They
all lie within five or six miles (8–9.6 km) of the town. Detailed
instructions on how to get to the starting point of the walk are
given at the beginning of each chapter.

■ Although not essential, because the walks are easy to
follow, the Ordnance Survey 1:25000 Outdoor Leisure Map of
The English Lakes, North West Sheet, Ennerdale and Derwent
will add much to the interest and appreciation of the beautiful
scenery that surrounds Derwentwater on every side.

■ Timetables of the Mountain Goat Bus Company and the
Keswick Launches can be obtained from the Tourist
Information Centre, which is situated on the ground floor of
the Moot Hall in the Market Square in Keswick.

Opposite: Lingholm and Causey Pike from Derwent Island

First Walk
Benjamin Bunny and Fawe Park

How to get there
Nichol End, the start of the Benjamin Bunny walk, can be reached in a variety of ways from Keswick.

■ *By car* Take the B5289 westwards from Keswick, towards Cockermouth, to join the A66 (Keswick by-pass). In a quarter of a mile (400 m) turn sharp left along the road signposted 'Portinscale'. Nichol End is half a mile (800 m) south of Portinscale village on the road to Grange (just after passing Derwentbank guest house). There is limited parking space by the track leading to Nichol End Marine, but this should not be relied on during busy holiday periods.

■ *On foot* Walk down Main Street from the Moot Hall and, immediately after crossing the river bridge, take the footpath on the left, signposted 'Portinscale'. In the village turn left along the road to Grange for half a mile (800 m). The total distance from Keswick is about a mile and a half (2.4 km).

■ *By bus* From April until the beginning of October the Mountain Goat bus between Keswick and Buttermere passes Nichol End. The company's office is in the Queen's Hotel, just below the Moot Hall, but the bus starts from the Central Car Park, near the back entrance to Woolworth's (from the Market Square go down the passage by the Oddfellows' Arms). The service runs two or three times a day.

■ *By boat* From the Spring Bank Holiday to the middle of September there is a ferry service between Keswick Boat Landing and Nichol End.

Opposite above: Nichol End Marine
Opposite below: Nichol End jetty

Beatrix Potter at Fawe Park

It was at Fawe Park that Beatrix Potter was staying with her parents in the summer of 1903 when she was preparing material for *The Tale of Benjamin Bunny,* and many sketches of the gardens appear in her Derwentwater sketchbook.

Before leaving London with her parents in July 1903 Beatrix had written to her publishers, Warne, on the subject of her next book. She said she had 'plenty in a vague state of existence' and continued, 'I had better try to sketch this summer, as the stock of ideas for backgrounds is rather used up.' The garden of Fawe Park clearly provided a more than adequate supply of ideas, for before long she wrote to Norman Warne, 'I think I have done every imaginable rabbit background, and miscellaneous sketches as well – about seventy!'

Although the Potters rented Fawe Park only for the summer of 1903, we can see from the Derwentwater sketchbook how important it was for Beatrix's work. The gardens slope down to the shores of the lake and have been landscaped to form

Opposite: The house at Fawe Park
Below: Part of the gardens at Fawe Park, looking rather bare in winter!

several terraces. Besides lawns and flower gardens, there is an orchard and a kitchen garden with greenhouses, cold frames and a potting shed.

Beatrix's artistic eye could see beauty in the hotchpotch of cold frames, garden implements, sheds and greenhouses, backed by the mellow brick walls of the garden. Probably in the first instance they were drawn for themselves alone, but we find them again, transmuted perhaps, as backgrounds to some of the scenes in *The Tale of Benjamin Bunny*. These watercolours are among the more finished pictures in the Derwentwater sketch-book; Beatrix obviously preferred the homeliness of the kitchen gardens to the more formal flower gardens which surround Fawe Park.

Greenhouses at Fawe Park, as sketched by Beatrix Potter (*opposite*), and as they are today (*left*)

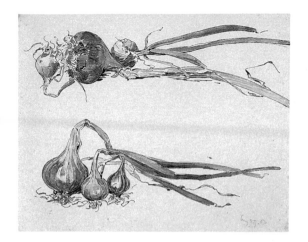

A selection of backgrounds painted by Beatrix Potter at Fawe Park in 1903, together with corresponding illustrations from *The Tale of Benjamin Bunny*

Above: Fawe Park photographed by Rupert Potter with the house just showing through the trees
Below: One of Rupert Potter's photographs of the interior of the house

It is perhaps surprising that there are no known sketches by Beatrix Potter of the exterior of the house at Fawe Park, which has some interesting architectural features. There is, however, a photograph by her father showing the house from a viewpoint along the shore of the lake. He also took several photographs of the grounds and of the interior of the house.

The Book

In *The Tale of Benjamin Bunny* we find Peter Rabbit and his more adventurous cousin, Benjamin, taking advantage of the absence of Mr. and Mrs. McGregor to climb over the garden wall, with the help of an overhanging pear tree, in order to rescue Peter's clothes, which Mr. McGregor has put on a scarecrow. Having retrieved Peter's coat and shoes, they proceed to steal some onions but are forced to hide under a basket to escape from a cat, which then settles down on top of the basket. The little rabbits are finally rescued by Benjamin's father, old Mr. Bunny, who sees the cat when he is walking along the top of the garden wall, smoking his pipe and looking for his son. He chases away the cat and sends Peter and Benjamin home in disgrace.

The Tale of Benjamin Bunny is full of scenes that can be traced directly to Fawe Park – the buttressed wall with a pear tree in the corner, the greenhouses and cold frames and the views across Derwentwater (*see the colour pages in the centre of this book*). Many of these features can still be seen today. The gardens of Fawe Park are not open to the public, but glimpses of them can be seen from a public footpath that runs beside the boundary fence and forms the main part of our first walk.

The Benjamin Bunny Walk

Starting point: Nichol End (G.R. 255228)
Distance: One mile (1.6 km)

From the road take the track that leads to Nichol End Marine, passing, on the right-hand side of the track, the private drive to Fawe Park (no public right of way).

The public footpath from Nichol End runs uphill to the right, behind the buildings of the Marine, crosses the drive to Fawe Park and continues outside the boundary fence. After a stretch of high stone wall, a section of wooden fence is passed, through which glimpses of the gardens of Fawe Park can be obtained. The top of the buttressed wall along which old Mr. Bunny walked (*see the colour pages*) can still be seen, and the pear tree by the wall looks old enough to be the one Benjamin Bunny and Peter Rabbit climbed down in order to get into Mr. McGregor's vegetable garden.

Those who feel frustrated by these tantalizing glimpses may sympathize with Beatrix Potter, who wrote to Norman Warne on 6 August 1904, when she was staying at Lingholm and *The Tale of Benjamin Bunny* was at the printers:

> I shall be very interested to see little 'Benjamin'. I tried to look over into Fawe Park garden the other evening and got all over tar, he might well have had that adventure in addition to his other scrapes!

The path continues downhill beside a wall, with a wood on the right. This must have been the wood where little Benjamin was sitting and where he found his cousin, Peter, huddled under a fir tree, wrapped up in a red cotton pocket handkerchief. There is a drawing by Beatrix Potter of Peter Rabbit's fir tree 'near Keswick' – perhaps the tree is still there.

Benjamin finds Peter Rabbit

A sketch of Peter
Rabbit's tree, together
with the finished
book illustration, and
an actual tree from
the Fawe Park Woods

When the path reaches the drive to Lingholm there are two choices.

(a) Return to Nichol End by taking the footpath through the woods that starts from the Lingholm car park (just above the Fawe Park path). The path leads uphill (still in Benjamin Bunny territory) and regains the Grange road a few yards from the Nichol End turning.

(b) Cross the drive and follow the Squirrel Nutkin walk, which starts by the main gate of Lingholm.

Whichever choice is made, it is well worth while visiting the gardens and woods of Lingholm, which are open on weekdays between 1 April and 31 October. Besides being the home of Squirrel Nutkin, the Lingholm woods were the scenes of many of Beatrix Potter's sketches.

Opposite: The return path through the woods of Lingholm

A squirrel in the woods around Lingholm, painted by Beatrix Potter in 1903, the year that *The Tale of Squirrel Nutkin* was published

Second Walk
Squirrel Nutkin and Lingholm

How to get there

The woods in which Squirrel Nutkin and Twinkleberry lived, in the grounds of Lingholm, can be visited as a continuation of the Benjamin Bunny and Fawe Park walk. If you wish to do this, refer to paragraph three, page 89. Otherwise, there are four ways to get to Lingholm from Keswick.

■ *By car* Take the B5289 westwards from Keswick, towards Cockermouth, to join the A66 (Keswick by-pass). In a quarter of a mile (400 m) turn sharp left along the road signposted 'Portinscale'. Lingholm is about three-quarters of a mile south of Portinscale village, on the road to Grange (past Nichol End and Fawe Park). The drive is on the left-hand side of the road, and there is a car park a few hundred yards along it.

■ *On foot* Walk down Main Street from the Moot Hall and, immediately after crossing the river bridge, take the footpath on the left signposted 'Portinscale'. In Portinscale village turn left and continue along the road to Grange for three-quarters of a mile (1.2 km). The drive to Lingholm is on the left. The total distance from Keswick is about one and three-quarters miles (2.8 km).

■ *By bus* From April until the beginning of October the Mountain Goat bus between Keswick and Buttermere passes Lingholm, stopping about a mile (1.6 km) further down the road at the Swinside Inn. Walk back down the road the way you came, to reach the drive to Lingholm on your right.

■ *By boat* From the Spring Bank Holiday to the middle of September there is a ferry service between Keswick Boat Landing and both Nichol End and Hawes End, both of which are within easy walking distance of Lingholm.

Beatrix Potter at Lingholm

Lingholm was the Potters' holiday home for many years – between 1885 and 1907 Beatrix and her parents spent nine summers there. In the earlier years Beatrix's brother, Bertram, accompanied the family on holiday, but by the time *Squirrel Nutkin* was published he had become an artist and spent long periods away from his parents and sister. Beatrix, therefore, was often alone and had plenty of opportunity for sketching.

The house at Lingholm is set in a large estate, with extensive gardens and woodlands that slope down to the shores of Derwentwater, giving Beatrix the freedom to wander in the woods and by the lake. The woods around Lingholm were – and still are – the haunt of red squirrels and other woodland creatures. Beatrix sketched them many times in the summer of 1901, when she was working on the backgrounds for *Squirrel Nutkin*. But although *Squirrel Nutkin* had already been completed when she started her Derwentwater sketchbook in 1903, the glades and lakeside bays, with their rocks and reeds, still held charm for her, and she continued to record them in her sketchbook.

Not only do we have Beatrix Potter's sketches of this area but there are also a number of her father's fine photographs showing

A page from Beatrix Potter's sketchbook in 1901, inscribed 'Wood near Lingholm used in Nutkin', together with the final book illustration

Owl and squirrel
sketches, 1901

Below: A sketch
by Beatrix Potter
of Derwent Bay

similar views. Many, especially those looking across to St. Herbert's Island (home of Old Brown, the owl) and Walla and Falcon crags on the far side of the lake, are easily recognizable today. The landscape has changed little since the Potters' stay, but trees that have grown up in the intervening years can sometimes make instant identification difficult.

The view of St. Herbert's Island from the shores of Derwent Bay is the same today as it was in Beatrix Potter's time, and it was obviously one of her favourite views, for the Derwentwater sketchbook contains several versions of it.

Opposite above: A view across to St. Herbert's Island and Walla Crag, photographed by Rupert Potter
Opposite below: St. Herbert's Island today
Above: Derwentwater sketched by Beatrix Potter in 1903
Below: The same view, in watercolour, from her 1901 sketchbook

Above: The gardens at Lingholm
Opposite above: Lingholm, by Rupert Potter
Opposite below: Derwentwater from Lingholm, by Rupert Potter

Lingholm, built in the 1870s, is a large country house needing several servants (at any rate in the Victorian era) to run it. During the last years of the nineteenth century it was generally unoccupied unless it was let furnished – as to the Potters – during the summer. Apart from a watercolour entitled *Rain, Lingholm, Keswick* and dated 'Aug., 1898' and an interior depicting a staircase (*see the colour pages*), Beatrix Potter seems to have had little interest in portraying the house at Lingholm, but her father took many photographs of it. He would have no difficulty in recognizing the house if he could see it today.

The formal gardens, which are now open to the public, were developed in the early years of this century, when the property was bought by Colonel George Kemp, later Lord Rochdale. The vegetable garden that Beatrix Potter referred to as a possible background for *The Tale of Peter Rabbit* no longer exists, but

A study of the kitchen garden at Lingholm, by Beatrix Potter

the woodlands that were the home of Squirrel Nutkin and his friends seem to have changed very little. They are open to visitors between April and October, and form the starting point of our second walk.

The Book

The Tale of Squirrel Nutkin began in September 1901 as a letter to Norah Moore, daughter of Beatrix's former governess and sister of Noel Moore, to whom the first Peter Rabbit picture-letter has been sent. 'A story for Norah' appears as a dedication at the beginning of the book.

In the story the squirrels sail across to St. Herbert's Island (called Owl Island in the book) with presents for Old Brown, the owl who lives there in a hollow tree, in exchange for permission to gather nuts on his island. Squirrel Nutkin, however, 'who had no nice manners', does no work and taunts Old Brown with riddles. Old Brown ignores silly Nutkin, impassively accepting the gifts brought by the other industrious little squirrels, until finally he can stand it no longer. He grabs Nutkin and pins him down, but the panic-stricken squirrel pulls himself free and escapes – minus his tail.

Lingholm, Keswick
Sept 25th 01

My dear Noah,

There are such numbers of
squirrels in the woods here. They
are all very busy just now gathering
nuts, which they hide away in
little holes, where they can find
them again, in the winter.

An old lady who lives on the
island says she thinks they come
over the lake when her nuts are
ripe; but I wonder how they
can get across the water? Perhaps

they make little rafts!

One day I saw a most comical
little squirrel; his tail was only an
inch long; but he was so impertinent,
he chattered and clattered
and threw
down acorns
onto my
head

I believe that his name was Nutkin
and that he had a brother called
Twinkleberry,
and this is
the story of how
he lost his tail —

There is a big island in the
middle of the lake covered with woods,
and in the middle of it stands
a hollow oak tree which is the
house of an owl, called Old
Brown. One autumn when the
nuts were ripe, Nutkin and
Twinkleberry, and all the other

"Old Mr B! riddle-me-ree?
(Nutkin bounced up & down and
clapped his paws)—
"Old Mr B! riddle-me-ree?
Arthur O'Bower has broken his band,
He comes roaring up the land;
The King of Scots, with all his power
Cannot turn Arthur of the Bower!"
Nutkin whisked and twirled and made
a whirring noise like the wind, and
flicked his bushy tail right in the
face of old Brown's whiskers.
Then all at once there was a
flufflement and a scufflement
and a loud "Squeak!!"

The squirrels scuttered away
into the bushes. When they came

back and peeped cautiously round the tree — there was Old Brown sitting on his door step, quite still, with his eyes closed: as if nothing had happened

But Nutkin was in his waistcoat pocket !!!

That is the end of the story. Old Brown carried Nutkin into his house, and held him up by the tail, intending to skin him; but Nutkin pulled so hard that his tail broke in two, and he dashed up the stair-case, and escaped out of the attic window.

And to this day, if you meet Nutkin up a tree, and ask him a riddle, he will throw sticks at you, and chatter his teeth, and scold, and shout — "Cuck cuck cuck cuck Currr."!

Yours aff Beatrix Potter

Beatrix Potter's letter to Norah Moore, 1901

Right: Norah Moore, 1900

The Squirrel Nutkin Walk

Starting point: The main entrance to Lingholm, opposite the car park (G.R. 252224)
Distance: One mile (1.6 km)

If the Lingholm gardens are open, a visit to them is strongly recommended, especially in April and May, when the rhododendrons are in full bloom (though some species continue flowering until July).

An entrance charge, in aid of gardening charities and the upkeep of the gardens, is made to visitors who, after passing through the main gate, will soon reach a stone plinth where the fee should be placed. From there the main route is indicated by white arrows, but, except where there are 'Private' signs, visitors are free to wander through the gardens and nearby woodlands. Eventually visitors will reach a sign, 'End of woodland gardens', and should return from there to the main entrance. There is a tea-room providing light refreshments, open from 1 pm to 5 pm (2–5 in April and October).

The Squirrel Nutkin walk starts along the public footpath to the right of the main gate to Lingholm, opposite the end of the footpath from Fawe Park, where the Benjamin Bunny walk finishes. It leads through woods that appear in many of Beatrix Potter's sketches, though the passage of time makes it difficult to identify any precise spot.

Emerging from the woods, the path continues across a field (which can be rather muddy in places), giving beautiful views of Cat Bells (the home of Mrs. Tiggy-winkle) to the left, and Rowling End and Causey Pike to the right, with the Newlands Valley in between. The path then leads through some more woods to a drive, signposted on the left 'Private drive to Lingholm Workshop, Derwent Bay House and Waterend House'. There is no public right of way down this drive, and trespassers will not be popular!

Opposite above: Lingholm Drive
Opposite below: In the gardens at Lingholm

Above: The Swinside Inn
Opposite above: Looking to Skiddaw from near Hawes End
Opposite below: St. Herbert's Island, from Derwent Island

Visitors who wish to return to Lingholm at this point should now turn *right* along the drive, regaining the road at Swinside Lodge. Turn right along this main road for about a mile (1.6 km) in order to reach the car park. On the way a road signposted 'Stair' leads off to the left, and a few hundred yards down this road the Swinside Inn provides refreshments during normal licensing hours. It is the only catering establishment in this area, apart from the Lingholm tea-room. The Mountain Goat bus stops at the Swinside Inn on its journey between Keswick and Buttermere.

Visitors who want to continue the walk, which finishes at Hawes End, should follow the footpath on the opposite side of the drive. This soon reaches another drive, where you turn left for a short distance, passing through a kissing gate. From this gate a path goes downhill through the trees to the landing stage, at which the Keswick launches call (weather permitting) every day from the beginning of British Summer Time until

the first Sunday in November. Launches travelling clockwise round the lake reach Keswick in ten minutes, while those going anti-clockwise take forty minutes.

The large island that can be seen from the landing stage is St. Herbert's Island, so called because in the seventh century, according to the Venerable Bede, St. Herbert, a saintly hermit, made his home there. He was a friend of St. Cuthbert, Bishop of Lindisfarne, and prayed that he might die at the same time as his friend. Bede records (though later historians disagree) that this wish was granted and that they both died on 20 March 687, an event that Wordsworth celebrated in verse:

> Though here the Hermit numbered his last day
> Far from St. Cuthbert his beloved friend,
> Those holy men both died in the same hour.

> *(Inscriptions XV)*

As mentioned on page 81, St. Herbert's Island is the Owl Island of *The Tale of Squirrel Nutkin*, the home of Old Brown. It now belongs to the National Trust and may be visited by hiring a rowing-boat or a self-drive motor-boat from Keswick, Lodore or Nichol End.

Third Walk
Mrs. Tiggy-winkle and the Newlands Valley

How to get there
The walk begins from the parking place at Gutherscale, about
3½ miles (5.6 km) from Keswick. You can continue from the
end of the Squirrel Nutkin walk by taking the path uphill to
the foot of Cat Bells instead of descending to the landing stage
at Hawes End. There are three ways to get to the parking place
from Keswick.

■ *By car* Take the B5289 westwards from Keswick, towards
Cockermouth, to join the A66 (Keswick by-pass). In a quarter
of a mile (400 m) turn sharp left along the road signposted
'Portinscale'. Go through Portinscale village and take the road
to Grange. The parking place is signposted from this road about
2½ miles (4 km) from Portinscale, just by the hairpin bend at
the foot of Cat Bells. A road runs from here to Skelgill Farm
(spelt in some places 'Skelghyll'), and there is a sign that reads
'Public Road. No parking. Parking 150 yards'. The parking
space is limited, however, and is liable to be full at holiday
times, so the following alternatives may be preferable.

■ *By bus* Take the Mountain Goat bus (only available from
April to the beginning of October) to Swinside Inn and walk
along the road towards Grange to the foot of Cat Bells and the
Skelgill turning, about half a mile (800 m).

■ *By boat* Take the Keswick launch
as far as Hawes End, walk up from
the landing stage to the road at
the foot of Cat Bells and then take
the Skelgill road.

Mrs. Tiggy-winkle at work

Beatrix Potter, the Newlands Valley and Mrs. Tiggy-winkle

The original Mrs. Tiggy-winkle was Beatrix Potter's pet hedge-hog, one of a collection of pets that often travelled with her when she went away. 'She enjoys going by train,' wrote Beatrix. 'She is always very hungry when she is on a journey.' This quotation comes from a letter to Winifred Warne, the niece of Beatrix Potter's publisher and fiancé Norman Warne, and was written on 6 September 1905, as *The Tale of Mrs. Tiggy-Winkle* was about to be published and less than two weeks after Norman's tragic death. The letter is embellished with a picture of the real Mrs. Tiggy-winkle drinking from a doll's tea-cup and with the familiar little figure from the story, dressed in her cap and using a knife and fork to eat her food.

The story of Mrs. Tiggy-winkle had, however, been planned as far back as 1901, and on the earliest known manuscript Beatrix Potter has written on the title page: 'Made at Lingholm, Sept. 01 told to cousin Stephanie at Melford, Nov. 01 – written down Nov. 02. There are no pictures, it is a good one to tell.' But fortunately Beatrix realized that it would be even better *with* pictures, and during her stay at Fawe Park in 1903 she made several sketches of the Newlands Valley and the mountain called Cat Bells that were to form the background to the story.

The evidence of her Derwentwater sketchbook shows that Beatrix Potter spent several days at least in the Newlands Valley, since the number of drawings, and their quality, suggests that they could not all have been completed at one time. Moreover, some of them are dated 19 and 21 September, which confirms this supposition. Five of the sketches are dated 15 September, indicating the speed at which Beatrix could work. There can be no doubt that in order to obtain her desired viewpoint the artist was prepared to scramble up the hillside and along rough sheep-tracks – in the warm sun and wearing the highly unsuitable garments of the period too. Even the ride out by pony trap from Fawe Park to Little Town must have taken

Opposite: Sketches of the original Mrs. Tiggy-winkle, Beatrix's pet

A sketch by Beatrix
Potter of 'the door in the
hill', and the finished
picture from *The Tale of
Mrs. Tiggy-Winkle*

Opposite: A boarded-up
mine entrance in Cat
Bells, which was
probably the inspiration
for this picture

some time and so curtailed the amount of sketching she could
do before her return. As a result, these sketches are not so
finished as those done in the vicinity of Fawe Park, but they do
have the freshness and immediacy of those fine autumn days
(*see also the colour pages*). One can still stand where Beatrix
Potter stood that September and look down over an almost
unchanged scene.

In Beatrix Potter's day a certain amount of lead mining was
still carried out in the Derwentwater area, and Beatrix remarks
in her *Journal* for 1885, 'It is a terrible place for drink . . . Every
fourth Saturday is the worst, when the miners are paid all their
earnings and go to the gin shop.' The paths to these mines, and
their boarded-up entrances, were probably the inspiration for
Mrs. Tiggy-winkle's house in Cat Bells.

The Tale of Mrs. Tiggy-Winkle is dedicated to 'The real little Lucie of Newlands'. She was Lucie Carr, the daughter of the vicar of Newlands and his wife, who lived in their vicarage in the hamlet of Little Town. In the book it is Lucie who goes up the Newlands Valley and finds Mrs. Tiggy-winkle, but the Lucie of the book is not exactly the same as the real Lucie . . .

For a start, Beatrix Potter decided that Lucie in the book should live 'at a farm called Little-town' – and what better name for a story about little people? Little Town does exist, but the picture of Lucie's home in *The Tale of Mrs. Tiggy-Winkle* is nothing like it – and exactly like the nearby farm at Skelgill as it is today, allowing for some modernization in the form of enlarged windows.

Sketch of Skelgill inscribed: 'September 13 '04', when the Potters were again at Lingholm. It is clearly the building shown as Lucie's home in *The Tale of Mrs. Tiggy-Winkle*

Opposite: Skelgill Farm today

Left: This pencil sketch from Beatrix Potter's Derwentwater sketchbook probably represents Little Town, as it was in 1903, but it was not 'the farm called Little-town' where the Lucie of the *Tale* lived. This was based on Skelgill, near Gutherscale, just over a mile to the north of Little Town

Below: Little Town and the lower end of the Newlands Valley today

The walk passes both Skelgill and Little Town, so walkers can judge for themselves where Lucie lived. She certainly seems to have started her expedition from a stile near Little Town. It seems that Beatrix Potter took the real Newlands Valley, moved it around and put it back together again to fit her story. It is a fascinating exercise in detection to identify the pieces and discover how they differ from the real landscape.

The Book

A little girl called Lucie has lost 'three pocket-handkins and a pinny' and walks up Cat Bells to look for them. She finds a door in the side of the mountain, opens it and discovers herself in Mrs. Tiggy-winkle's kitchen. Mrs. Tiggy-winkle, 'a very short, stout person', is a washer-woman. She is ironing a batch of clothes, including Lucie's lost articles. Together they deliver the clean laundry to its small animal owners, and Lucie returns home. She looks back to see the washer-woman has gone – 'Why! Mrs. Tiggy-winkle was nothing but a HEDGEHOG.'

The Mrs. Tiggy-winkle Walk

Starting point: The parking place at Gutherscale (G.R. 246212)
Distance: 3 miles (4.8 km)

From the parking place, walk along the road as far as the gate of Skelgill Farm and then take the path that continues ahead, just above the wall of the farm. This path runs along the lower slopes of Cat Bells and on a clear day gives magnificent views of the fells surrounding the Newlands Valley: Maiden Moor, Hindscarth, Robinson and Causey Pike are the principal ones. The view behind is almost equally striking, with the great mass of Skiddaw rising above the slopes of Swinside. This view appears in the book picture of Mrs. Tiggy-winkle giving the birds and mice their nice clean clothes.

Opposite above: Newlands Valley and Causey Pike
Below: Swinside and Skiddaw, near the start of the walk.

Left: A sketch from Beatrix Potter's Derwentwater sketchbook of a crag in the Newlands Valley, known locally as Castle Nook

Below: Spoil-heaps of the old lead mines

The path continues along the wall until it crosses the spoil-heaps of the old Yewthwaite lead mines, long since abandoned. High up under the summit of Cat Bells some of the open shafts can still be seen. The most dangerous of them has been boarded up since a fatal accident in 1962, but there may well have been a proper door there in Beatrix Potter's time.

From the spoil-heaps the path crosses the bed of a stream by a wooden bridge and bears right, following another wall, towards Little Town. Just past the last house the track bends sharply downhill to the right, and a gate leads on to the road.

If time and energy allow, it is worth making a detour, before following this downward path, by taking a track to the left that runs up the beautiful Newlands Valley. One of the illustrations in the *Tale of Mrs. Tiggy-Winkle* shows Lucie on this path, which continues for several miles to the head of the valley. Not far away, the little white church of Newlands, where the real Lucie's father was vicar, can be seen in its group of trees.

Newlands Church

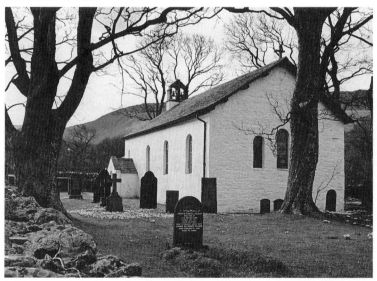

To continue the walk, retrace your steps to the downward path and descend to the road.

On reaching the road at Little Town, turn right and continue along the road, which shortly passes the Newlands Vicarage. Just after a steep hairpin bend a white house, Ghyll Bank, is reached on the right. According to the Ordnance Survey map the right of way leads through the gate of Ghyll Bank, but a notice on the wall just past the house directs the walker to a permissive path about 20 yards (18 m) further up the road, where a stile leads into a field.

The path runs diagonally left across the corner of the field to another stile and gate and continues across the next field. The lie of the land prevents the next stile from being seen, but aim for the tallest tree and the stile will be found nearby. Beyond the stile the path follows along a fence, which is on the left, goes through a gate and passes several cottages to the buildings of Skelgill Farm.

Turn right uphill through the farm buildings, and regain the road to the car park through the gate.

Ghyll Bank

Above: Swaledale sheep at Skelgill farm, with Skiddaw behind
Below: The towering landscape between Ghyll Bank and Skelgill

Epilogue

BEATRIX HEELIS was determined to preserve the beautiful
countryside that had been her inspiration since those first
holidays by Derwentwater and where she spent the later years of
her life. In her will she left 4,000 acres of land, including fifteen
farms, to the National Trust, thus helping to ensure that visitors
to the Lake District today can enjoy the largely unchanged
country in which she walked and sketched and which formed
the background to her most famous books.

Above: A sketch of Hill Top by Beatrix Potter, 1905
Opposite: Beatrix Potter at Hill Top in 1907

Select Bibliography

The Journal of Beatrix Potter, 1881–1897. Transcribed from her code-written manuscript by Leslie Linder (Frederick Warne, 1966)

Beatrix Potter's Journal (*abridged*), Glen Cavaliero (Frederick Warne, 1986)

A History of the Writings of Beatrix Potter, Leslie Linder (Frederick Warne, 1971)

The Derwentwater Sketchbook, 1903, W. Bartlett and J. I. Whalley, limited facsimile edition (Frederick Warne, 1984)

The Art of Beatrix Potter, Leslie Linder (Frederick Warne, second edition, 1972)

The Magic Years of Beatrix Potter, Margaret Lane (Frederick Warne, 1978)

Beatrix Potter, Artist, Storyteller and Countrywoman, Judy Taylor (Frederick Warne, 1986)

Illustration Acknowledgements

The authors and publishers would like to thank the following for their help in supplying illustrations. Page numbers are given, except for the colour illustrations, which are referred to by their caption numbers in **bold** type.

Aerofilms: **1**; Wynne Bartlett: pages 64, 66, 96, 99, **4**, **10**, **19**, **22**, **29** and **32**; Winifred Boultbee: page 39 *(right)*; John Clegg: page 51 *(above)*; David Garland: page 51 *(below)*; Trustees of the Linder Collection: pages 17 *(below)*, 33 *(above)*, 35, 37, 50, 68 *(below right)*, 69 *(above left* and *below right)*, 73 *(above right)*, 77, 79 *(above right)*, 92, 98 *(left)*, 109, **7**, **11** *(above)*, **12** *(above)* and **20**; the National Trust: pages 26 *(below)*, 81 *(below)*, **14** *(left)*, **15** *(left)*, **16** *(left)* and **17** *(left)*; Robert Thrift: pages 56, 57, 58, 60, 62, 65, 73 *(below)*, 74, 80 *(below)*, 83, 88, 90, 91, 100 *(below)*, 102, 104 *(below)*, 105, 106 and 107; Victoria and Albert Museum (the Leslie Linder Bequest): pages 14, 16, 17 *(above)*, 18, 19, 20, 21, 23, 25, 27, 30, 31, 32, 33 *(below)*, 34, 41, 47, 68 *(above left)*, 70 *(below)*, 76, 78 *(left)*, 79 *(above left* and *below)*, 81 *(above)*, 84, 86, 87, 94, 97 *(right)*, **5** *(right)*, **6** *(right)*, **11** *(below left)*, **19** and **30**; Frederick Warne & Co.: pages 13, 24, 26 *(above)*, 28, 29, 38, 39 *(left)*, 42, 43, 44, 45, 52, 53, 54, 55, 67, 68 *(above right* and *below left)*, 69 *(above right* and *below left)*, 70 *(above)*, 71, 72, 73 *(above left)*, 75, 78 *(right)*, 80 *(above)*, 82 *(below)*, 85, 93, 97 *(left)*, 98 *(right)*, 100 *(above)*, 101, 104 *(above)*, 108, **2**, **3**, **5** *(left)*, **6** *(left)*, **8**, **9**, **11** *(below right)*, **12** *(below)*, **13**, **14** *(right)*, **15** *(right)*, **16** *(right)*, **17** *(right)*, **18**, **21**, **23**, **24**, **25**, **26**, **27**, **28** and **31**; Jonathan Wolstenholme: page 48.

Index

References in *italics* denote illustrations; there may also be textual references on these pages. References in **bold** type refer to the numbered colour plates. Beatrix Potter is referred to as BP.